BUSY WOMEN STRESS LESS

Stop Stress without Overeating

Breaking Free to a
PEACEFUL MIND

30 Stress Days ~ 30 Insight Solutions

Patricia A. Ronzio, M.Ed.

New Paradigm Wellness Publishing

P.O. Box 200789, Austin, TX 78720, USA

512-244-6292

Email: coach@newparadigmcoaching.com

www.newparadigmcoaching.com

ISBN: 978-0-9903464-1-8

Table of Contents

Foreword

I have known Patricia Ronzio for more than 25 years and in that time, I can truly say she has been a guiding light in my life. My admiration for her continues to grow, she doesn't simply develop concepts of how to live a fully balanced life, Patricia is one of the few people I know who actually "walks the talk."

For as long as I have known Patricia, I have been in awe of her focus and rise in relation to her career as a professional health and wellness director. Her work with her husband Dr. Robert Ronzio, (The Encyclopedia of Nutrition and Good Health), combined with her outstanding skills as a successful independent personal and professional coach and her abilities as a professional speaker, are all underpinned by her natural abilities to inspire, empower, transform and teach.

I have had the amazing privilege of being coached by Patricia, during different times in my life and have been deeply enriched from her guidance and expertise. I have personal experience of using the "Insight Empowered Stress Management" approach outlined in this "Busy Women, Stress Less Series" of books.

I know from personal experience, that it's not enough to simply understand the insights gained from life's lessons, although these are truly important and the first step to creating change in our lives. However, where Patricia shows true brilliance is taking us one step further by linking general "stressors" of everyday life that we experience and linking these with "insight inspired action." It is her ability to co-pilot us into action that I find truly momentous.

Patricia's new concept of utilising a "Wellness Blossom" map as a way of systematically looking at the full flowering of potential, is based on her own remarkable experiences of bringing her life into balance. Her profound understanding of the common stressors we face as women along with our emotional needs are all tackled in this series of books. It's like finding "communication" gems all in one place, without having to go down a mine shaft to find them.

As an example, in Day 1 of this book, Patricia introduces us to one of the most important stressors I struggle with in my own life, that of saying "No" and guides us to engage with boundaries around this. Her recently quoted, "if no is not an option, yes is not a choice," is being actively used as a guide in my daily life choices.

I am very privileged to be working with Patricia in her role as an international coach and heartily recommend this book as an essential tool in achieving a peaceful mind.

Freda Lacey,

Mental Health Officer, Voluntary Council, Wales (United Kingdom)

A New Credo to Help You Stop Stress (without using food)

Get Ready to Discover Your Own Best Stress Solutions

- Are you tired of sacrificing your health and happiness when stress at home or at work leaves you feeling overwhelmed?

- Do you want answers to nagging problems that keep you awake at night?

- Are you frustrated by simplistic, off-the-shelf formulas, tips and "secrets" that promise stress relief?

- Are you ready to discover the ultimate customized stress management approach?

If your answer is YES, you have come to the right place!

I am convinced you can find lasting solutions because I know this for sure ...

- You are creative, strong and powerful

- You are your own best expert for your life

- You can stop the stress response without overeating

The *Busy Women Stress Less Series*™ is devoted to helping you manage stress and meet life's challenges. This four volume series, *"Stop Stress without Overeating: 30 Stress Days: 30 Insight Solutions"* shows you how to spark your own creativity to find personal stress relief in meeting life's challenges without overeating.

Why I Wrote These Books

I had a decades-long weight problem. I started dieting when I was 11 years old. At one point my weight crept up to 230 pounds. [In England where I lived, that was equivalent to 16.5 stone]. The yo-yoing up and down, the on again/off again diets seemed to indicate I was weak-willed.

I thought I was to blame for repeated failure with diets and that I didn't have any willpower, even with success at school - top scores in class work, elected class prefect and Head Girl.

The pivotal moment came when I realized I didn't have a weight problem – I had a stress problem!

Stress taught me four principles that became foundations of the *Busy Women Stress Less Series™*.

#1. Each of us is unique.

#2. We can trust our inner creative genius.

#3. Real solutions embrace our entire being.

#4. We never fail, we simply get feedback as to what works and what doesn't.

An Empowering Approach to Lasting Stress Relief

I have lived through struggles with self-confidence, self-criticism, out-of-control eating and frustration. I have stumbled and skinned my knees and eliminated blind alleys, to discover success on the other side.

I will show you how I used creative problem solving to resolve everyday hassles and energy drains that so many women face – again and again. Thirty "case examples" describe very real solutions for very real problems taken from my own life. These very same problems are familiar to women and occur repeatedly in my coaching practice.

Along with decades of experience as a life coach, an educator and a background in corporate wellness, I developed a very practical stress management system to:

- Simplify problem solving

- Save you time trying to eliminate blind alleys and detours that I had to deal with

- Provide you with a practical step-wise process, which you can practice daily

- Help strengthen your self-confidence

The *Busy Women Stress Less Series*™ is not for everyone. If you want rigid rules or simplistic solutions - you will not find these here.

What you will get are real life applications of insights and creativity to transform very common stressors. Discover how to find your own successful stress solutions to manage chronic stress without overeating.

Insight-Empowered Stress Management™ [IESM]

The IESM employs Insight-based problem solving, to empower you and encourage your creativity.

Do you remember when you suddenly found the answer to a perplexing problem, when a missing piece of the puzzle fell into place? Can you recall how good that felt?

You still have that ability, and with encouragement and guidance, your "insight muscles" can grow stronger. You will be amazed at the number of options that can open up in front of you.

If you are like me, creative problem solving – including letting my mind wander, using intuition, and coming up with "crazy ideas" - was not encouraged in school or in my work life. That is so ironic! Each of us is born with the ability for "out of the box" thinking.

Simplify Problem-Solving with the Wellness Blossom Concept Map

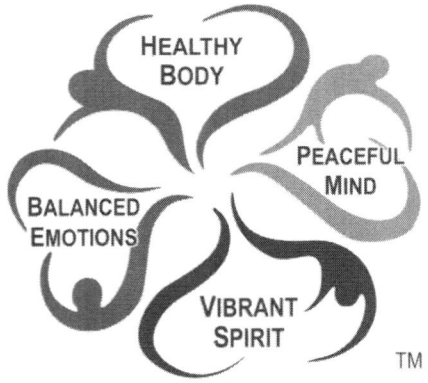

The second strategy of the IESM is to use the Wellness Blossom as your trusted guide as you explore new territory.

The Blossom emphasizes my holistic approach. It has four Petals:

- **Healthy Body Petal**
- **Peaceful Mind Petal**
- **Vibrant Spirit Petal**
- **Balanced Emotions Petal**

Each represents a different wellness domain. The Blossom helps you break things down into manageable chunks to allow you to pick and choose what to do.

Explore Insight Solutions within the Peaceful Mind Petal

The **Peaceful Mind Petal** reminds you of beliefs, thoughts, values, or biases that shape learning, memory and perceptions.

Thoughts are a breeding ground for chronic stress. Disturbing thoughts can create stress. Have you heard the exclamation, "I don't want to open a can of worms?" This idea goes back to the conventional stress model in which the brain interprets input – from thinking, experiences and our senses – to generate emotional and physiological stress responses.

Quick Assessment: Where Do You Stand in the Peaceful Mind Petal?

To clarify focal points for this Book, below are five questions to help assess your overall strengths, and identify specific topics that you may wish to explore. (There is no "right" or "wrong" answer, there is only what is real for you right now.)

1. I am aware of an "inner critic" and speak gently to myself. (Yes, No, or Maybe-sometimes?)

2. I have healthy personal boundaries, and know how to set limits with other people. (Yes, No, or Maybe-sometimes?)

3. I possess strong self-esteem. (Yes, No, or Maybe-sometimes?)

4. I am assertive, not passive, in my relationships. (Yes, No, or Maybe-sometimes?)

5. I like the person I see in the mirror. (Yes, No, or Maybe-sometimes?)

Stress Begins in the Brain

The Downside: Negative thoughts can get in the way of creative problem solving and lock us into emotional responses to stress that may have been embedded by childhood experiences. Outdated thought patterns intensify chronic stress, and a downward spiral of not enough sleep, compromised eating, inadequate exercise and self-care and feeling blue or irritable.

The Upside: Thoughts can be changed, leading to lasting stress relief. With examples from my own life, I will show you how to identify chronic stress-promoting thinking, and how to generate fresh insight-inspired solutions that counter unhelpful thoughts, beliefs, biases, or viewpoints.

How to Benefit from the Peaceful Mind Petal

Turning to the Wellness Blossom concept map, the **Peaceful Mind Petal** embraces topics such as how we communicate with ourselves and with others. It includes negative/positive self-talk and clear interpersonal communication. This Petal asks you to consider your assertiveness skills, your ability to set and maintain healthy boundaries, as well as attitudes that influence responses to potentially stressful social settings. A Peaceful Mind embraces a strong self-esteem and self-confidence.

Let's get started!

Unlock chronic stress... your creative genius is waiting! Here are two ways to begin:

- Ready for a month of stress breakthroughs? You can choose day-to-day insight building beginning with Day 1 in the Table of Contents.

- You can also use the Table of Contents to select a stress theme as it comes up.

Each day can provide a springboard to the exciting world of Insight-Empowered problem solving, beginning now! This is about changing the habits of a lifetime, really focusing on where the sticking points are, and setting yourself free so that you never need to stress eat again.

Prepare yourself for an exciting adventure. I would love to hear how insights help you stop stress without overeating at: coach@newparadigmcoaching.com.

To your creative stress solutions and personal empowerment!

Patricia

Austin, Texas, U.S.A.

How to Use This Book

I have organized each entry systematically, to demonstrate a logical sequence of problem-solving steps. Daily entries describe a real life, stress-related issue.

Stress Point

I began with a very specific problem that many women face. Stress points are usually easy to identify: They seem to defy resolution, despite everything you have tried. They are chronic stressors ... energy drains that go on and on.

- You may lie awake at night with worries that will not go away, problems that seem to defy answers and leave you exhausted mentally and physically.

Insights

Here I illustrate "Aha's" that came to me after stepping back from the immediate issue.

- New ideas and perspectives develop and your creative genius shines through, when the brain is given time: Time to make connections and find innovative approaches to the problem. Time for gratitude, realizing blessings and the gift of Life. Time to connect with a Higher Power and the Divine, according to individual beliefs.

Insight-inspired Actions

Stay-awake-at-night problems can be amazing starting points for insight building. Insights can generate multiple solutions (like butterflies emerging from cocoons), and I describe steps used to explore several options.

- When your actions are insight-inspired and driven by your inner creativity and genius, you make connections that lead directly to the outcome you seek. Your insight-inspired actions open the door to change. Without action, stress persists. Without action, nothing changes.

How This Worked

This section explains how insights helped me reduce stress without resorting to eating when I was not hungry, and it describes the ramifications of new choices.

- Solutions that work long-term are those that come from your own answers to handle your unique challenges. Whether or not actions give you the exact result you wanted, you can confidently learn from the experience without guilt.

Insight Builder

Ready to delve deeper into a given topic? This section provides an expanded context for insights about immediate stressors.

- I have taken a global approach, with comments on how these issues affect women in America, as well as in other countries. This international perspective may assist you in exploring related topics for further insight discoveries.

Question

Each daily topic concludes with a question intended to assist you in considering aspects of your own stress point in a different light. The outlook from the top of a mountain is often more revealing than viewpoints in deep valleys.

Day~1

Healthy Relationships: How to Say "No!"

I overheard our three year old grandson in the living room talking to himself. Curious, I paused to listen before entering. Imagine my surprise when I realized the little guy was repeating the word "No" using every inflection he could imagine...a soft No, a whining No, an angry No! Around and around he went, practicing his elocution with hand gestures. I withdrew to honor his privacy. Wow, this kid is on to something.

Stress Point

Do you remember a nursery rhyme that goes something like this: "Sugar and spice and everything nice, that's what little girls are made of?" I grew up with the unspoken guideline that girls should be "nice." The details do not matter as much as the fact that I continued this way of relating to others well into adult life.

Insights

What a shock to discover how often the "Yes" word seemed to fly out of my mouth almost automatically, in response to requests from a friend, family member or people I wanted to impress. There had to be a way to create time to think before committing precious time, energy and brain cells to someone else's priorities, demands or expectations.

Insight-inspired Actions

With awareness of an entrenched 'yes to be nice' pattern and realization that "if no is not an option, yes is not a choice," it was time to honor "me."

Egregious requests: A "No" response comes more easily here – such requests and demands are simply out of the question. Period! I have other immediate priorities; I am leaving tomorrow; I have already told you no, and so on.

Requests that are potentially doable: These can be tricky, because time is needed to think through ramifications and find an appropriate response. There is an easy way to push the pause button and interrupt automatic responses without over-thinking the situation. Rather than being pressured into a quick yes or no answer, I use phrases such as "I'll get back to you on that tomorrow" or "I'll think about it."

How This Worked

How often do we say "yes" to a request when our inner voice, our heart, wants to say "No?" A "yes" response may offer the path of least resistance, especially when we're tired, upset or afraid. Yet acquiescing to be nice can set up internal conflicts and stress, and eventually harm health and well-being.

Postponing a decision even for a few minutes can create enough mental space for the rational mind to kick in, to weigh the pros and cons before deciding how to answer. There is time to ask:

- What's my comfort level with the person or situation?
- Do I feel manipulated or controlled?
- Does this situation nurture me, and will the outcome support my growth?

11

Insight Builder

A request to volunteer services or to take on extra responsibilities can be a fresh opportunity to honor our personal preferences and values. Pushing the pause button can help us stay true to goals and maintain strong interpersonal boundaries.

In the organizational world, requests can provide opportunities to explore and negotiate alternatives. Does this request make sense? Are there more appropriate alternatives? Is this the best option for all parties involved? Which trade-offs affect self-care, family and relationships? In other words, what are the potential benefits and what is the potential downside?

Question

Beyond early indoctrination about how girls should behave, does saying "yes" help us find recognition, approval and praise from those whose opinions matter? Is saying "Yes!" a shortcut to feel safe and more loved?

The next time circumstances suggest you "should" say yes to a request from someone to whom you feel obligated, can it become an opportunity to explore your thoughts, preferences, beliefs and expectations?

Day~2

Critical of Your Partner? Part 1: Dealing with 'Dumb' Mistakes

Do you become upset when your partner or spouse makes "silly" mistakes? Perhaps he or she misspelled the name of a restaurant, purchased the wrong brand of laundry detergent, or gave you an incorrect URL? Perhaps your partner made a wrong turn by refusing to research directions ahead of time. It's as if there is an internal radar screen set to catch offenders. What action will we take when they are "caught?"

Stress Point

I have an excellent eye for details. When someone makes a mistake in speaking or in writing, I can flag it very quickly. While this trait is an advantage in editing and record keeping where accuracy is a premium, it can be a complication for personal relationships, especially in dealing with my spouse, family and friends.

Insights

This issue is about me, not my partner or family member. Irritation or impatience are my territory. That is what I have control over and can change. I cannot control or guess at the behavior, thoughts and emotions of anyone else.

Some mistakes have important consequences, such as altering closing costs on purchasing a house, or misunderstandings that exacerbate deeper issues. In these situations, it is time for clear and respectful communication to negotiate a winning solution.

Insight-inspired Actions

Before commenting on another's perceived error, I ask myself: What specifically would I like to be different and what actions can I take that will honor this relationship?

I can request clarification since I may have misinterpreted the action/inaction: "This is what I heard, is that what you meant to say?"

When I am sure what I heard was accurate, I may continue the conversation, while keeping my tone of voice neutral and avoiding blame or guilt. As an example of a door opener: "Are you open to hearing some feedback?" If the answer is yes, explore ways to create a deeper understanding and collaborate to resolve the problem.

How This Worked

Often we jump to conclusions based on faulty information or old familiar patterns. Therefore an early priority is listening carefully to what my partner is saying. Though I might relish correcting a mistake and "win" an argument, this approach seldom strengthens a relationship or builds trust.

If my partner is not in a mental space to hear constructive feedback, I can share how the current situation impacts me directly, together with a suggestion on how to work together to change it. Self-righteousness does not nurture personal growth. My heart seeks growth within personal relationships. The need to be right does not fulfill that desire, nor does it bring fulfillment.

Insight Builder

Isn't it ironic that people may treat strangers with more patience and understanding than their own family members and those whom they profess to love? Does neglect in building or maintaining a relationship, indicate that a partner is being taken for granted? Perhaps the relationship has become stale, uninteresting and automatic.

Question

Does your tolerance level for a partner's mistakes vary according to your mood or stress level? What does this say about perceptions of "right" and "wrong?"

———————————

Day~3

Critical of Your Partner? Part II: Dealing with Irritating Habits

Sometimes it's the repeated little idiosyncrasies that can get under our skin when we live with another person. Old Ego may feel gratified in detecting faults. What then?

Stress Point

It came down to the newspapers. My husband often reads today's newspaper over coffee during breakfast. No problem with that. However, by receiving national and local printed news, papers can accumulate rapidly – dining table, chairs, window ledge -- what have you. Sometimes he cleans up after reading, at other times distractions pull him away and disarray persists.

Insights

I always have a choice about how to respond to behavior traits. Attempt to change me, or attempt to change him. How about stepping back to look at the situation from the outside?

Insight-Inspired Actions

There are starkly different options for dealing with someone's annoying habits:

Option 1: The "you are bugging me – stop it!" approach. Sounds like a blame game, doesn't it. People don't like to be accused or made wrong.

Option 2: If a behavior pattern is inconsequential, I can ignore it in the context of a broad perspective. (The incident does not change fundamentals: I love him/her. I have far more important priorities today.)

Option 3: I can communicate my discomfort to my partner using the "I message" formula, which can go something like this, "When you do [blank], I feel [blank], and I need to work out a solution with you to deal with this."

How This Worked

Committed relationships offer multiple opportunities for disagreements and misunderstandings. Patterns that do not conform to our values or preferences can trigger judgment, which translates to annoyance. How can we handle habits like leaving laundry in the washing machine? Not filling the tank with gas when it's close to empty? Letting dirty clothing accumulate? Being late for appointments?

Insight Builder

Criticism and a need to be right in relationships are age-old life challenges. Why are the mistakes of others so glaring and vexing?

There are positive alternatives to impatience and aggravation when we notice another's faults: We can choose to become mindful of our thoughts and values that make their actions objectionable. Isn't the wisest choice a commitment to work together to resolve any shared sources of stress?

Question

What chronic behaviors in others do you find annoying? Are you satisfied with your responses to these patterns? How might you improve the situation to lessen the impact of another's annoying trait?

Day~4

Managing Stress and Multi-Tasking: Are you a Duck or a Tuna?

There are times when my mood bounces around according to entries in the event calendar. A day may be filled with a whirlwind of tasks, each competing for precious minutes. Am I going to be like a duck bouncing up and down with the waves and paddling like crazy to get ahead, or am I going to be like a deep sea tuna, swimming calmly beneath the waves and unaffected by the turbulence overhead?

Stress Point

Okay, I lost it -- totally overwhelmed, frustrated and on the verge of tears. It was one of those days when the stars, planets or whatever guides daily events present one problem after another. Too much to do, minutiae that takes me away from more important work, leaving me frayed and short-tempered.

Insights

Multi-tasking stress shifts me away from creative problem solving and a balanced evaluation of pros and cons. It short-circuits personal relationships. I end up putting out brushfires, instead of strategic planning. To get back on track, I need to think creatively about meeting the next challenges with a systematic approach to calm jangled nerves.

Insight-inspired Actions

How serious is the situation? Does it warrant a call to 911? Nope! Does anyone require outside assistance? No again. Great! Let's move on:

1. *What is the most stress-inducing task you face right now?* How does that stressor affect your thinking, mood or physical symptoms?

2. *Stabilize the "patient."* This is an instance when a quick fix can actually help. The point is to return to a balanced, centered state. Because overwhelm represents an acute stress response, do whatever seems easiest and most effective to get your heart rate back to normal: Breathe deeply and slowly. Listen/watch a creative visualization. Take a hot bath or shower. Get a massage. Go for a walk. Find a quiet environment for a healing prayer or meditation. Things like that.

3. *Strategize ways to successfully complete necessary tasks.* A proven approach is to pull up the top five tasks, prioritize them in terms of urgency and impact, and then schedule time to complete them, according to their importance. Scheduling can help change apparent chaos into order. It puts you back in control, with less time in reactive stress, and more time in creative, insight-driven problem solving.

How This Worked

An underlying assumption for various published stress scales is that in a reactive mode, stressors pile on top of each other. We end up working harder just to stay afloat. With a proactive mindset, we feel calm and confident, armed with clear goals and a plan of action. Deadlines, conflicting tasks, and time crunches scarcely disturb us.

Insight Builder

Research over the last decade indicates that simultaneously carrying out challenging tasks can reduce productivity by up to 40 percent. Research also suggests that some people (5-10 percent) may be able to multi-task comfortably. Some workers may be able to handle two simultaneous and routine tasks that do not require a lot of problem-solving.

Women may yield to expectations about assuming a multi-tasking role – maintenance of a household and childcare, together with the additional responsibility of providing a family income.

Question

Is this an opportunity to slow down, to stand back and determine how comfortable you feel about what you have been taught about a woman's role, and what you think you need to do?

———————

Day~5

Journal Writing to Nurture a Peaceful Mind

Recording life experiences in a diary is something our mothers or grandmothers may have done. Likewise letters to a pen pal, poetry and other creative writing are established outlets for expressing thoughts. Women today have additional options for personal expression, such as blogging, in addition to personal journal writing.

Stress Point

Today my head is filled with jumbled thoughts that lack a coherent pattern. They tumble about like clothes in the dryer. Now this thing comes to mind, now that. It feels like a random brain dump. Help!

Insights

Journal writing becomes a tool to get to know thoughts, ideas and actions that can bolster self-confidence. Identifying disturbing thoughts decreases the intensity of related negative emotions. Beyond logging events, exploring thoughts and feelings through writing can be an effective stress reliever.

Insight-inspired Actions

Get a grip, Patricia! You need to be focused if you want to stay on today's tight schedule.

However, unlike the clothes dryer, which stops tumbling when I open the door, ideas and thoughts in my head don't stop when I say stop.

How about trying a new tactic to create space to sort out individual thoughts, one by one?

Okay, sounds like you are willing to create "Me time" to work on this, even when doing so takes take time away from projects.

A starting point: Find a quiet spot, a peaceful environment, where you will not be interrupted. Inventory thoughts, ideas, feelings and insights one by one as they occur to you. There is no need to prioritize them or "analyze" them.

How This Worked

Journal writing contributes to a Peaceful Mind. I become measurably calmer and happier than before. As I record thoughts, jumbled ideas download like computer files. My mind opens up and my vision becomes clear. Solutions to problems emerge from fresh awareness and new insights. It's like giving my creative side a helping hand.

Insight Builder

Due to the stress of pressing schedules, it is often difficult to generate creative solutions. Journaling provides an outlet. I release what is bothering me. I can review individual events, and discover interconnections. For these reasons, journal writing has become a pillar of my self-care practice.

The act of writing, whether with pen and paper, a word processor or an iPad, converts something as ephemeral as ideas into tangible stepping stones. Several published studies indicate that keeping a journal helps individuals clarify goals, sort through options, and discover fresh insights regarding weight management, among other challenges. Other research suggests that regular journaling can bolster immune cells (lymphocytes) and reduce inflammation associated with asthma and arthritis.

Question

Today, can you write a letter to a make-believe sister or your closest friend, to share the details of the most troubling stress point you face? Tomorrow, feel free to throw it away, because your subconscious will have had time to work with this new reality and spark fresh insights.

Day~6

Is it "Clutter" or is it A Way of Life?

Clutter is a subjective term, isn't it? While it may not seem that clutter has anything to do with a peaceful mind, the two are related in an important way.

Some individuals tolerate messiness while others cannot live in a disordered environment without enduring stress. The central question is how each person engages clutter. Some may view a space (office, garage, bedroom, and so on) as filled with distractions, while others may see the same area as interesting, even inspiring.

Stress Point

My husband and I have very different views of clutter. I have a well-honed sense of order at home (and at work). What constitutes a messy house? Important items are not in their "rightful" place. Instead they are helter-skelter, and I end up feeling resentful of time wasted attempting to find a needed item.

Bob has a much more laissez-faire attitude toward clutter. Somehow he manages to keep track of stacks of papers, books and scribbled notes "scattered" about his workspace. Oh! Oh! A coat, old newspapers and reading materials can gradually encroach on the dining table, sofa and living room.

Insights

Personal items scattered throughout the house contribute to my unease, erode a sense of balance and increase stress levels. An additional complication: litter catalyzes overeating. The more clutter I see, the greater the temptation to visit the kitchen and nibble on leftovers to temporarily restore balance.

Insight-inspired Actions

Clutter in personal areas? Bob has his work area and I have mine. Because disorder may trigger stress eating, it is essential that my office is ordered and tidy to my heart's content. Likewise, Bob's office organization reflects his preferences and comfort level.

Clutter in shared areas of the home? Compromises help each of us to get needs met. The living room and family room are prime examples. We agree to put away personal items, such as reading materials, by the end of each day. We provided adequate storage for cluttered items: a shoe rack at the entryway handles exercise shoes and walking shoes. A closet is set aside for the vacuum cleaner, attachments and cleaning materials.

How This Worked

For me, a sense of order is linked to a desire for peace of mind. It was surprising to discover a link between messiness and stress eating. At first glance it made little sense to link the two together.

Making sure each important item has its own "home" helps to counter feeling out of control. Occasionally when I am very busy, clutter accumulates, emotional equilibrium begins to tilt toward stress, and a desire to overeat resurfaces. Those signals alert me to "clean up and put away." My partner honors and supports those efforts.

Insight Builder

During graduate school I recall two faculty members with adjacent offices. Professor A took pride in having an immaculate desk. Book shelves carried journals arranged neatly by year. Reports were always stored in file cabinets. Current projects were centered on her desk. Students tagged her office, "Cleanliness is next to Godliness." In contrast, Professor B's desk was littered with correspondence, manuscripts, stacks of books and journals, which often spilled out onto the floor. Students had labeled this office, "A little dirt never hurt anyone." Who was "right?"

Question

I propose that each of us carries an internal scale for assessing "clutter," whether or not this scale is used consciously or unconsciously. What happens when your internal scale registers 'too messy?' More importantly: Does your physical environment at work or at home reduce your stress level, or does it add to your stress load?

Day~7

Criticism and Praise: Two Sides of the Same Coin?

You have organized a dinner for friends and family – a relaxed, informal, get-to-know-you-better event. Guests are obviously enjoying the party, with one exception, who grumbles about the food, the entertainment, or about other guests. Do you find yourself preoccupied with accommodating the one dissenter?

You've done a good job, perhaps an outstanding job with your workshop or class. Most of the attendees' evaluations are complimentary. Then you detect a negative qualifier – someone has criticized, or demeaned your performance. What comes next?

Stress Point

I had driven four hours to Corpus Christi on the Gulf Coast to give a breakout session on stress management. The professional audience was attending a two day workshop on improving wellness in the workplace.

The presentation went smoothly, I felt energized in making the presentation interactive, and attendees seemed fully engaged. After collecting written evaluations, I surveyed the results. Many attendees gave the session a high [excellent] rating, though one was derogatory.

Would negative feedback ruin my day?

Insights

It is amazing how often the mind wants to skim over positive feedback and focus on negative news. Preoccupation with negative feedback can trigger self-recrimination, with thoughts such as, "why didn't I do better?" or "why didn't I see that coming?" Self-criticism fails to nurture self-confidence. I can reverse negative thinking with a reality check.

Insight-inspired Actions

I prepare for an objective evaluation. In a quiet setting I scan the evaluations, noting positive comments and any negative feedback. A detailed analysis of results can guide future presentations.

How This Worked

To obtain an objective assessment after public speaking, it is useful to consider both positive comments and negative feedback, especially constructive criticism. Both types of feedback can yield insights for improving presentations, in terms of content, clarity, pacing, relevance, question/answer opportunities, handout materials and the like.

In a non-business setting, there are several proactive options. Did I hear the criticism accurately? If the criticism does not affect other guests, does anything actually need to be fixed? Is there an opportunity here to look at how the criticism triggered my "hot buttons?" In any case, worry about one person's critique can become a downer for the party.

Insight Builder

Positive feedback is nuanced: It is natural to desire to be accepted and praised. However, audience "likes" come with caveats. For formal settings, positive feedback can be helpful when it is anchored with specific, perceived benefits. Did an audience take away the intended message, or did they respond to a "minor" point or side bar?

Informal settings are more fluid and feedback can be more subjective – based on impressions and interpretations that can come and go.

Negative feedback comes in different flavors as well. In formal settings, feedback from colleagues (peer review) can be very useful when it reveals weaknesses, blind spots and errors. When corrected, the overall quality of a presentation or report may be significantly improved, in accord with your goals. An ability to learn from critique can actually inspire creativity at work.

Question

In either formal or informal settings, how do you respond to positive and negative feedback?

_____

PEACEFUL
MIND

Day~8

Is Noise a Hidden Stressor?

Astronomers worry about the effects of "light pollution." As urban areas have grown, light emitted from those centers interferes with star gazing and limits data collection. Can you name another source of pollution that broadly alters life in the 21st century? Yes! The culprit is Noise.

Stress Point

I work from a home office overlooking oak trees, expansive lawns and limited cul-de-sac traffic – all in all, a peaceful working environment. I also take periodic breaks from the desk and computer, to stretch and step outside for a taste of nature. So what is the problem?

The world has a way of intruding when I need to relax. A chronically barking dog. A neighbor who revs up his sport bike and roars down the street. Things like that.

Insights

Loud, repeated noise can startle me. Instant anxiety can trigger a food craving. It was time to be proactive and tackle those unsettling noisy disturbances.

Insight-inspired Actions

Noise sources I can influence?

Something mundane: The alert signal from my smart phone. I muted the ringer to a soft chime.

The sport bike ... Stopped the rider. With a neighbor, I described how his speeding and muffler-free machine posed a hazard (and was not street legal).

The barking dog ... Contacted the dog's owner. Met to describe how her dog barked for hours apparently out of boredom while she was away at work.

When other outside noises interfere with relaxation on the patio, I move to another area. A fountain and pond are a short distance away, for example. When a lawnmower revs up, there are always ear protectors.

How This Worked

Although eating temporarily alleviates stress, whatever the source, it provides no permanent resolution to noise-induced stress. The key to stopping the stress response in this case lies in changing the environment – eliminating the noise source when possible, blocking it out if necessary.

Insight Builder

Noise represents a mind-altering form of pollution. It seems the busier we are, the greater the risk of extraneous noise. There is traffic noise. Calls via smart phones. Neighbors noisy interactions. Ramped up MP4 players and favorite music clips. Noisy household appliances. Is that hubbub really harmless "white noise"?

Excess noise creates ear damage and impacts our brains. Vibrating air molecules can interfere with neurological

32

pathways responsible for interpreting information as well as cognitive processes like problem solving and memory.

Question

Hearing is often taken for granted as one of the five senses, yet noise can subtly affect mood as well as thoughts. How many distinctive sounds can you identify at home, at work, or outside? How many of those are restful? Which do you find disturbing?

———

Day~9

How to Improve Self-Confidence: Inspiration from a High Wire Walker

I recently viewed a video clip of Nik Wallenda crossing the Grand Canyon in Arizona on a cable strung across the chasm. At a distance of 1,500 feet above the canyon floor (no safety net!), he made crossing look easy. What was a key to his remarkable success? Total self-confidence! And how had that come about? Extensive practice and commitment to a vision!

Stress Point

A critically important interview was fast approaching. It was the career-making kind, offering a significant step up the corporate ladder - with more interesting responsibilities, more opportunities for professional growth, more fun, and a compensation package that indicated the company was seriously committed to employee well-being. I needed to ace the interview.

Insights

Could I learn something from this high wire walker? The most striking aspect of Wallenda's achievement was his mental attitude and commitment to practice. He was absolutely convinced that he would complete his challenge easily. This guy practiced in his backyard to such a degree that he felt calm walking across a cable, whether it was strung 4 feet above the ground, or suspended above the Colorado River. He employed a wind generator to mimic the effects of winds blowing across a practice cable, stabilized by dangling weights to limit swaying. And he used an immense balance bar to maintain a low center of gravity.

Insight-Inspired Actions

Like a high wire artist, I imagine moving easily back and forth around a balance point, visualizing each step leading to the next success, and imagining the thoughts and emotions that accompany those successes. To prepare for contingencies and remain confident in gusty winds, I employ trusty stress management techniques in a self-care toolkit to help maintain equilibrium. These include meditation, qigong, yoga and an enjoyable exercise program. Guidance from spiritual readings. Practicing interview questions. Recalling previous successes. Consulting a trusted support network of friends and family members. Using positive affirmations.

How This Worked

Centering is like finding a safe harbor, a calm inner place where we can view our actions and challenges with equanimity. Attempting to be centered 100% of the time is unrealistic. Centering does not rely on inflexible rules and schedules for success. Instead, it can be viewed as a dynamic process supported by a repertoire of reliable practices to relieve stress.

Insight Builder

The most corrosive form of stress is the chronic and persistent, nipping at the ankles, wear you down kind. Thoughts and related feelings rattle around in our heads like popcorn in a popper. Chronic stress can feel like walking across an unending, swaying rickety bridge that threatens to plunge us into a chasm at any step. Beyond altering mental equilibrium, chronic stress unbalances metabolism, setting the stage for premature aging and difficult-to-cure chronic diseases. Holistic approaches to benefit self-confidence are powerful antidotes. Paying attention to our physical, mental, spiritual and emotional well-being nurtures the belief, "I can do this!"

Here are several effective strategies to help you remain confident under trying circumstances. Take time to discover which of the myriad stress reduction techniques work best for you.

1. Repetition, i.e. practice, helps develop skill sets to overcome adversity and improve performance. Practice requires commitment and consistency, independent of a quick reward.

2. Plan ahead and anticipate challenges – what could go wrong?

3. Take more action to gain momentum, without worrying about perfection.

4. Surround yourself with positive and understanding individuals. Peer support can bolster your self-confidence.

5. Stay true to your values, to being true to yourself, to keep holding your vision of what you want to achieve.

Question

When facing a challenge at home or at work, what are the most effective ways to help you strengthen self-confidence? When was the last circumstance in which you felt completely self-assured?

Day~10

How to Reduce Commuting Stress

Who hasn't experienced commuting stress due to drivers who tailgate, speed regardless of posted limits, use bright headlights at night, cut you off from a traffic lane, or run through red lights. What can we do about the indignation and resentment they trigger?

Stress Point

It's rush hour. Like almost everyone else, I am completely focused on getting home after a challenging workday. Traffic is 'stop and go' along the usual stretches of the highway. Suddenly the driver of an SUV swerves into the lane in front of me, accompanied by yells and gestures. I brake, hoping the driver behind me is alert enough to avoid crashing into my car. I arrive home more stressed than when I left the office!

Insights

The first impulse was anger resulting from the threat of an accident and being subjected to male aggression. These thoughts led to feeling defensive and wanting to yell back.

This incident offered a choice point: I could choose an angry thought process, or I could use this incident as an opportunity to take care of myself.

Insight-inspired Actions

I have no control over the thoughts or actions of other people. However, I do have control over my responses. I like to use a simple mantra when individuals challenge my sense of fair play. "Peace be with you, I am at peace."

How This Worked

While my ego can be indignant at the apparent failings of others, such judgment brings no peace. My judgments "you're wrong!" provide endless "teachable moments" to restore a sense of calm and harmony, when I am ready to re-center, think clearly and creatively. Less blame for him! More peace for me!

Insight Builder

It is time to renew defensive driving skills for safety. Time to be more alert to motorists who are fatigued, who are speeding or driving erratically, who use smart phones to call or text, who are preoccupied with children, who are mentally not with it, whether due to medications or other influences. It may be time to consider changing commuting routes and times, to reduce congestion and mental wear and tear.

Question

If "inconsiderate" drivers enter your life as opportunities to grow, what can you learn that will help you be more considerate, patient, or more peaceful?

Day~11

Quit Your Job or Stay?

Beyond a steady paycheck and meaningful work, employees often seek job satisfaction. a complex mix of recognition, career growth, and support of basic values. And yet, recent surveys suggest that as many as 52% of professional women in the U.K. are dissatisfied at their workplace.

Stress Point

After working for an international organization for several years in London, I was no longer satisfied. True, I had accumulated seniority and the salary was excellent. This position could be considered a "plum."

A growing unease at work, negative thoughts about the company and a diminished role created high level stress. Dissatisfaction with work reached an all-time high. Clearly, this position had become professionally untenable.

Insights

Continuing with my current employer was no longer feasible. Would I limit my options: find similar employment in London, or would I consider changing careers, even changing countries if that turned out to be the very best choice?

Insight-inspired Actions

A job search revealed several opportunities abroad. Choosing one of those options would require cultural adjustments, in addition to adjusting to new responsibilities and a new institutional environment. This triggered anxious thoughts that could have held me back from taking a leap into the unknown. Am I good enough? Will I burn all my bridges? How will I stay connected to family and friends?

What is real here? I allowed those negative thoughts to come and go without being attached to them. After carefully weighing the pros and cons to move to Canada I decided to pull the plug. I submitted my resignation and emigrated, choosing to broaden my skills in a different line of work and to be free from very real limitations.

How This Worked

It was important to give negative thoughts "air time" without allowing them to become real and paralyze me. Remaining at the old position would have kept me "small." Several coworkers confided that they wished they had the courage to break free. In leaving an apparently dream job, I dramatically expanded horizons of what was possible. By taking a calculated risk in severing old lifelines I opened the door to a new life, more fulfilling than I had ever dreamed possible.

Insight Builder

Many of us change jobs or residences multiple times over the span of decades. New opportunities for advancement, a changed economic picture, midlife reassessments, or empty nests can provide an impetus to seek solutions when the old ways no longer work.

A recent survey of employed women in Europe found them to be more exposed to psychological stressors than men, even among Europe's most progressive regions. These pressures include high job demand with low job control and low social support; and high effort coupled with low reward as compared to male counterparts.

New career paths provide multiple opportunities for change. The choice to leave a job is strengthened by evaluating the pluses and minuses of continuing on with the same position versus finding new sources of income.

The European Labor Market offers new opportunities for workers, yet they must be flexible to take advantage of different types of jobs in different regions. A 2006 study found that one third of E.U. citizens had moved to alternative job markets. While their U.S. counterparts were typically staying 4.6 years at a given job, a median of 80% of Europeans considered conditions for the local job markets to be "bad" (2012).

Christopher Reeve summed it up best. "Either you decide to stay in the shallow end of the pool or you go out in the ocean."

Question

How many times have you changed jobs? If you were to choose your "dream job," how would it differ from what you are doing now?

———————

Day~12

A Key to Stop Overeating - No More 'Ms. Doormat!'

Frequently overeating can be a symptom of stress due to unresolved relationship issues. A doormat syndrome is characterized by acceptance of someone's criticism, letting others "walk over" our personal space. Doormats often feel powerless. Though such hurtful behavior is the antithesis of love and acceptance, it may be endured to varying degrees for years or decades.

Stress Point

During my first long-term relationship my boyfriend expected me to cook dinner every night. I did not like to cook, and I had little experience with it. Consequently I didn't perform this task well. Criticism of my cooking skills gradually became more destructive, with zingers gradually leading to tantrums and food hurled at the wall.

Insights

One of the traits linked to allowing partner abuse was a need to be responsible for keeping those close to me calm and happy (not angry!). The tip-off: I felt horrible inside, yet fearful of confronting him.

Insight-inspired Actions

Drawing upon friends and prayer, I found the strength to terminate that abusive relationship. I packed my bags and walked out the door forever.

I understand now that overeating helped numb the pain of hurtful interactions with this individual. I had been unable to confront his destructive behavior because of old thinking patterns. I had hoped that intimacy, closeness and love would come by complying with a partner's definition of my role. Fundamentally, this was an old belief that love can only come with hooks.

Before getting involved in another relationship, I focused on identifying self-limiting beliefs, while acknowledging inner strength and self-worth.

How This Worked

An initial step toward healing began with realizing that there was a huge relationship problem and that drastic action was required to break away from such ingrained patterns. While consultation with qualified healthcare providers may be required, journal writing can be an important step in reviewing incidents, identifying associated negative thoughts and feelings and excuses for abusive behavior. Overtime, with encouragement and support, I learned how to stand up for myself. "I deserve unconditional love, and I will not tolerate abuse." Very powerful intentions!

Since that time long ago, I have created a supportive marriage where cooking, and other aspects of a mutually supportive relationship are shared as joyful experiences. There is no need to overeat during meal preparation or afterward.

Insight Builder

Verbal abuse as hostility can show up as withholding love, ignoring or belittling your ideas, wishes and desires, refusing to acknowledge your input, or hypercriticism of minutiae. Anger can become a manipulative tool. The abuser may act out of a need to feel superior, to dominate and control, due to his own shortcomings. Often abusers go to great lengths to cultivate a "good guy" persona in a social circle, where complaints may be met with disbelief and the opinion that you are the one who needs help!

How often do we consider evaluating thoughts and beliefs about those who seek to limit us? Perhaps we write off daily events as small disturbances, as something we can live with. We may hope that a partner will eventually change for the better. Sometimes we rationalize hurtful behavior by saying he is doing the best he can, given his circumstances -- hallmarks of enablers, who acquiesce to hurtful behavior.

Lasting change relies on identifying the traits that left the door open to abuse. Often they relate to low self-esteem and weak personal boundaries. Professional counseling may be required to help turn the corner and recover from deep hurtful experiences.

Question

Are there recurrent situations at home or at work in which you feel resentful, disempowered or hurt? How would you like circumstances to be better? What action will you take to make that happen?

Day~13

How to Change "I Can't" to "I Can" ... with a Phillips Screwdriver

"If you think you can do a thing, or think you can't, you're right." - Henry Ford

How often does our mental chatter reflect statements such as "I'll never be able to do "ABC." Or, "I always mess up with "XYZ." Or, simply saying 'I can't!'

Stress Point

I open a box containing new cable attachments for the TV. The instruction manual is gibberish. Illustrations do not match described steps, themselves disordered. Taking my best guess to hook up the device, I turn it on. No control works. What next?

A sense of discouragement and defeat creeps in, followed by mind chatter, "I'll never be able to get this to work!" A choice point: do I repack the box in disgust and grab a comforting snack? Or do I rise to the challenge?

Insights

Walking away meant that I was trapped by a self-fulfilling prophecy! There has to be another way, I just hadn't found it yet. Hundreds, no thousands of women have connected cable networks and DVD/VCR to their TV's. I can do this!

Insight-Inspired Actions

I will not give up. Instead, I take the instruction manual outside to peruse it in the peaceful environment of the garden and then call customer service for clarification of the puzzling steps. Note when tools such as a Phillips screwdriver are needed. (Who is Phillips?)

Follow my notes and new instructions to make all connections. Install batteries in the remote. Plug in the device. Voilà, everything works perfectly. Here's to success in a mechanical world!

How This Worked

Long, long ago, in a land far way, a school girl was required to explain Archimedes' Principle to her fourth grade class. When she failed to meet the male teacher's rigid criteria, he humiliated her before the entire group with sarcasm and disdain. Lesson learned: She can't do physics or math. Get it wrong and suffer the consequences. That got etched into my psyche!

Self-limiting statements, such as 'I can't,' are examples of irrational thinking, and like a bunker on a golf course, they can trap us in a variety of ways:

- Lock us into old automatic and self-limiting responses

- Block our innate creativity

- Reiterate harmful or self-destructive behavior, including overeating and bingeing

Insight Builder

Technical mastery can serve as a metaphor toward achieving a Peaceful Mind in a world that is being revolutionized by technology and human connectivity.

We live in an increasingly technical and mechanical world, which seems to foster a dependence upon outside "experts." Service calls may offer us easy solutions when appliances and machines malfunction and wear out. In contrast, mastery of basic repair and maintenance offers independence (beyond savings on repair bills). Familiarity with common tools such as hammers, pliers and screw drivers confers self-reliance that goes back to our pioneer roots.

Question

Whatever challenge brings you frustration today, to what degree does the thought, you "might not be good enough" to solve the problem, augment stress? What steps can you take to change that perception?

———————————

Day~14

How to Maintain Clear Boundaries (Especially with Those You Love)

Aunt Marian was a dear soul - good humored and never one to gossip or complain about others. Family members naturally congregated at her home during holidays. While we lived in the vicinity, we too gathered at Aunt Marian's.

Everyone contributed a dish, however this was Auntie's day to shine. She was an amazing cook. Some of my fondest memories came from the delicious aromas from her kitchen. In particular, Aunt Marian was proud of her Shepherd's Pie, featuring a recipe handed down through generations. Tasty, absolutely! It came with one little problem.

Stress Point

- Aunt Marian: "Oh look, your plate is empty. Have some more …."

- Me: "Um, no thanks, Auntie. It's delicious, but I'll need room for dessert."

- Aunt Marian: "How about just a little more. You must still be hungry after such a long drive."

- Me: "No thanks, Auntie. I've had enough and I really don't want more."

Insights

Personal boundaries represent key elements of self-care, and their practical application can affect interactions during mealtimes and beyond. With Aunt Marian, I wanted to make my intentions clear, gently and firmly, while acknowledging and sincerely appreciating her efforts.

Insight-inspired Actions

To continue the conversation:

- Aunt Marian, walking over with the serving tray: "You're sure you won't have just one more dollop?"
- Me, holding up a hand: "Auntie, it is as wonderful as always. But I don't want to eat any more right now. Let's save it for tomorrow."

The boundary, "No thanks, I've had enough," related to my preferences, not to the quality of Auntie's cooking. She may have pouted; she may have wagged her finger at me. How Auntie responds is her territory, not mine.

How This Worked

"Mothering" is not confined to mothers when food is equated with giving and sharing love. How often have we been admonished with, "Eat, eat, there's plenty more where that came from!"

We may acquiesce to avoid embarrassment, or to avoid hurting a loved one's feelings. However, saying, No! can help maintain an internal equilibrium, and prevent unwanted consequences, in this case too many extra calories and weight gain.

Insight Builder

Where do we draw the line between acceptable and unacceptable behavior? A sense of obligation can color our interactions, particularly when we have a long relationship history. We may not want to disappoint them or "hurt" their feelings. Sticking to boundaries becomes trickier when we want to be cared for too. The immediate question is how to survive when food means love?

Question

If you feel uncomfortable setting a boundary with a relative whom you love, can you identify related thoughts, preferences and beliefs? How are those beliefs serving you?

———————————

Day~15

Eating "Mindfully" ... Time to Examine Our Thoughts?

How often have we been told to "Stop it" or "Just get over it," with "It" being stress-related behavior like overeating or splurging. Admonitions such as these are entirely off base. As a counterbalance to simplistic advice, we possess powerful skills that can help us break free of an overeating/dieting mindset.

Stress Point

It is mealtime and out of habit I grab a plate and utensils for the table. Open the refrigerator. Heat up the dishes in the microwave. Get something to drink. Sit down to eat. Then inevitably ... a flurry of thoughts:

Wait. Forgot to get the mayo out of the fridge – I need to remember to buy more. Hmm, this is breast cancer awareness month - I'll touch base with Sylvia. Uncle Pete did not sound well over the phone - I want to send him a get well soon card. Mind chatter continued.

Pushing away from the table, I glance around. Dishes and utensils in the dishwasher and hunger relief are the only indications that I have actually consumed a meal. Savor it? No way. Not even sure how much food landed on the plate!

Insights

Central to being assertive is eating with awareness of thoughts, beliefs and attitudes. In other words, we can choose to eat mindfully rather than on autopilot.

Insight-Inspired Actions

How to slow down racing thoughts and switch to feeling peaceful, fully aware of the food on my plate? Foods themselves provide clues. I tune into the aromas, textures, flavors, and appearance of each offering. This is a beginning.

Then I tune into current thoughts before picking up a fork. When they are distractions, I can counter them with an affirmation, a blessing, or a prayer along with eyes closed and slow breathing. Now I'm ready to eat!

How This Worked

Rather than following simplistic advice such as "stop eating so much," or yielding to veiled criticism with associated guilt, such as "stop being a pig," it is far more empowering to consider thoughts and feelings that accompany mealtimes.

With busy daily lives, we may shift to default mode, eating automatically, unaware of the rich experience a meal can provide. Deep down we understand that unconscious eating does not satisfy, however habits can trample that awareness.

Stopping a stream of thoughts and internal commentary, I begin to see, smell and taste foods. Fully aware, there is no need to eat more than necessary to satisfy hunger. I enjoy meals more and end up eating less.

Insight Builder

All too often simplistic solutions for healthy lifestyle change do not come from individuals who have experienced the stressors under discussion, nor have they personally experienced related stress responses. Advice givers often come across as insensitive, short-sighted, superficial and paternalistic.

Question

Have meals become single line entries in your scheduler rather than serving as highlights of your day? Have you examined thought patterns while eating, for example during a "power" lunch? How do those thinking patterns affect meal-related stress?

———

Day~16

Eldercare and Giving Advice - Her Stress or Ours?

Eldercare has become much more common as Baby Boomers pass midlife and discover their parents and older relatives are living longer. Caring for them creates a dilemma: What kinds of recommendations should we provide when we feel certain that our advice will help improve their health, safety and possibly enhance their well-being?

Stress Point

I kept in touch with the family's "grand dame" as she became frail and the years rolled by. Gram, I would say, have you thought about being a little more active, you know, to keep flexible? Some people I know use gentle forms of yoga to help them relax and to reduce morning stiffness. (Gram would say, "Hmm.") I would like to send you a cool book on yoga for older persons. It shows how to use easy postures – no need to sit cross-legged on the floor. (Gram would say, "well okay!")

On other occasions I gently coaxed her to think about certain nutritional supplements, explaining that with age, intestinal absorption declines and nutrient needs can increase. Vitamin B_{12} is an example. Gram, I would like to send you some supplements to try out. Of course, check them out with your doc. Gram would say, "Go ahead and send them, I'll look them over." Follow up calls met with her response, "I'm still thinking about it."

When Gram passed away, relatives began the task of cleaning her home of decades of accumulated "stuff." I was shocked to discover that health books I recommended had been stuffed in a box in the basement. The nutritional supplements I sent were stacked, unopened, in a bathroom cabinet.

Insights

In retrospect, Gram had not exactly asked for advice. I had acted on my interpretation of what her lifestyle "should" be. Unused books and bottles, was there a lesson for me? It had been so obvious. I had been convinced that if Gram would take some anti-inflammatory supplements and essential nutrients and if she would commit to a regular movement program, her stamina and health would improve. Yet, she had chosen to ignore advice and gifts.

Insight-inspired Actions

Although it is difficult to detach from a loved one's personal choices, the bottom line is this: if I am stressed when my advice is not followed, that is my problem, not the recipient's.

How This Worked

Gram's formative years spanned the Great Depression and World War II. Physical exercise, supplements, and self-help books were not part of her paradigm, nor did her generation focus on aspects of self-care we now take for granted, such as communication skills or couples counseling. She was not about to change, despite well intentioned relatives. She felt most comfortable with what she knew, including conventional medicine and prescription medications.

Insight Builder

From parents and role models we acquire fundamental beliefs about personal health, relationships, career – you name it. Those attitudes and beliefs help define a woman's role and aspirations. However, when we reach beyond that comfort zone, one or more of those beliefs can stop us in our tracks.

Question

How does attachment to giving a loved one advice about health and lifestyle change serve you? And where does tolerance of their choices enter the picture?

Day~17

Dealing with Perfectionist Goals: Can Broccoli Help?

Religious and national holidays and celebrations can stimulate a renewed commitment to cleaning up our lifestyle, particularly after excesses at the dinner table and vegging out afterward.

We know we should be doing more to take care of ourselves, to eat better and get more exercise:

- "I am definitely going to give up sugar and eat more vegetables. Please pass me the broccoli and Brussels sprouts."

- "I'm going to activate my gym membership and start exercising an hour every day."

- "That's it! No more cream cheese (or coke or potato chips)."

Stress Point

I'm going to get rid of the excess weight that has been bugging me, and I promise to keep it off! I am totally serious about losing weight this time.

I study the new diet plan as if preparing a research paper. I purchase a beautiful journal to log foods and calories for each meal, including snacks and beverages. I ruthlessly discard all foods excluded by the diet plan. I let people around me know – this time is for real!

Insights

Focusing on extreme measures satisfies a perfectionist, self-righteous part of my brain. Then reality asserts itself. Eventually – a few days, a couple of weeks, perhaps even after a month or two – I waiver in the face of obstacles. Maybe I eat a food not allowed on the diet. Or I forget to note a treat or two or three on a food/calorie log. Perhaps I couldn't determine the number of calories in a multiple ingredient dish a family member had prepared. One thing leads to another and I end up thinking, "That does it, this diet can't work," and I give up. What is worse, a sense of guilt and failure overtakes me.

Insight-Inspired Actions

It is time to restore insight-building and a reality checker. Let's focus on a renewed commitment to a healthy lifestyle and weight management beyond dieting. I want to simplify, so I will stick to improving food choices.

Many published guidelines note that consuming more veggies can have a significant impact on reducing the risk of chronic disease such as Type 2 Diabetes. To make this change easier, how about eating more vegetables that I enjoy? Steamed broccoli is at the top of my favorite vegetable list, which includes baked yams, pickled organic cucumbers along with mixed veggie soups.

How This Worked

Dieting reinforces a false sense of being in control of life. Attempting to follow a diet plan perfectly and permanently sets me up to fail. In sharp contrast, focusing on progressive steps to eat more healthful foods feels empowering, it is do-able, I feel better and have a lot more fun.

Insight Builder

Is an "all out" single leap health goal an act of desperation? Though fear is a potent motivator, does it lead to a realistic appraisal of what can be accomplished? By committing to idealistic or impossible lifestyle changes, we may yield to a need to be perfect, while setting up roadblocks to the very thing we want to accomplish.

Selecting achievable and insight-inspired goals increases the odds of success. The strength of a personal commitment is a further ingredient for successful lifestyle change. Research indicates that the probability of keeping a promise to change increases dramatically when the commitment is documented or witnessed.

Question

If you were to commit to a single lifestyle change beginning today, which core beliefs and ideas support such a change? Which thoughts would tend to drag you down and drain needed energy to be successful?

Day~18

How to Stop Self-Criticism: Lessons from a 'Twin Sister'

Birth twins often have special relationships. Studies demonstrate that twins' lives are often intertwined in profound ways, and those connections may last a lifetime. I contend that most of us possess an internal "twin" who is with us from birth to death, a twin who persists in looking over our shoulder.

Stress Point

I named my "twin" Angie. I love Angie, I really do. She knows all my quirks and I know hers. Internal twins can assume many guises, and Angie has this maddening trait: she is super critical. While my critical twin occasionally dozes, at other times she is ever so ready to pounce on any apparent transgression or error. When I make a mistake, or don't live up to an expectation, Angie shouts derogatory terms at me like, "Dummy" or "Stupid" or "There you go again!"

Insights

An internal negative voice has been labeled - Inner Critic - though I believe this phenomenon is far more personal. Derogatory comments from Angie make me feel terrible. Awake at night, thinking of solutions to my Angie dilemma, a light bulb switches on: If I don't talk to myself kindly, how can I expect others to treat me any better?

Insight-inspired Actions

It is time for a very frank conversation with Angie. I dig up photos taken when I was two years old and place them on the office wall. When I hear that scolding twin, I look over at those toddler photos and ask, "Angie, that little girl does not deserve blame, does she? Doesn't it always hurt her?"

How This Worked

Angie and I, we are that little girl posted on the wall. Oh yes, she's still with me! It is my responsibility to treat Angie with the utmost love and respect. She secretly understands this truth, and she snuggles up close.

Insight Builder

The weight of judgment can feel overpowering at times. Negative thoughts spur negative emotions, limit creativity, shut down love and block progress toward a given goal. The best antidote is to treat my inner twin with the tenderness and love that she craves.

Question

External criticism, such as put downs and the like, can be forms of veiled aggression, and therefore are hurtful. Are you aware of hurtful self-talk patterns? Will your inner commentary nurture the little girl? If not, what other words would you choose to convince her that she is loved?

Day~19

Ambushed by Stress After Work?

You may have heard that old adage, "Leave the work at work." Easy to say, but hard to accomplish! Work-related stress can follow us home, taking the guise of pending deadlines or new managerial responsibilities.

We look over at the passenger seat on the drive home, and what do we see? Ms. Stress. We arrive home, and as we open the front door, Ms. Stress sidles in. Will she tempt us to eat beyond satisfaction to deal with the lingering tension?

Stress Point

Work was demanding, however I felt that I was on top of my workload. Not feeling great, but okay. Feeling stressed? Nothing out of the ordinary …

Arriving home after work, I began to unlock the front door. Bam! Tension literally swept me through the doorway into the house. Desperate, all I could think of was food, food, food! I headed for the kitchen to sample whatever I could find in the fridge.

Insights

A work-binge cycle continued until I understood the connection between work-related stress and overeating at home. I needed reliable techniques to avoid being ambushed by work stress.

Insight-inspired Actions

It was a relief to take a direct approach to such a persistent and frustrating energy drain:

- I ate a healthy snack before leaving work.

- After leaving the office I sat in my car for a few moments to become aware of any tense or tight areas in my body. I listened to soothing music while driving.

- Upon arriving home, I avoided going to the kitchen. Instead I went straight into the bedroom to put on my exercise clothes and running shoes. Then I walked through the neighborhood for at least half an hour.

How This Worked

I made sure I did not arrive home hungry. Calming activities reduced a need to eat. By walking after work, I was able to process niggling thoughts. Invariably, tension dissipated. No longer preoccupied and feeling more peaceful, I was able to think clearly about dinner, and how I would use the rest of my evening constructively.

Insight Builder

Travel back in time with me: As an employee, my father never brought work home. When 5 pm or 6 pm rolled around, he and his coworkers closed up shop. Working on weekends? Did not happen! My mother and father had plenty of time for hobbies, family activities, civic projects and travel. All while working full-time and doing more than meeting job expectations.

Switch to the present. Surveys indicate that Americans are working harder and longer than their forebears, perhaps reflecting economic downturns and the rise of double income families. Many skip vacations, which can seem to be luxuries. Or they take work along in the form of laptops and hand held devices to stay connected. Figures for the U.K. and America are similar. In contrast, several other nations report much higher work hours per person. These include Taiwan, Singapore, Republic of Korea and Hong Kong.

In addition to economic factors and societal or cultural work ethics, other factors may be involved. For some people the workplace can be a sanctuary where expectations are predictable, clearly defined and "safe," while a home environment with its mega responsibilities can produce the most stress. For others, a job can become an important source of personal validation and peer recognition.

Question

Does your job compensate for shortcomings in the home environment, or vice versa? If you choose to make work and home life more fulfilling, what steps would you consider for stress relief? Is this an opportunity to prepare an action plan?

Day~20

'Mistakes' - Real or Illusions?

Do you sometimes resent people's "dumb" mistakes that cost you time or money? How about when comments, made out of spite or ignorance, left you embarrassed or resentful? We may complain to friends who are willing to commiserate, when we seek confirmation of our judgment. We may say things such as, "Would you believe (he, she, they,) did not ...?" Or, "You would think that (he, she, they,) would have ..."

Stress Point

It is a day when nothing seems to be going right. Moody and stressed, my tolerance level is bottoming out. During breakfast and while commuting, I fret about what "they" did (or did not do). Negative thought following negative thought. Not a good day!

Insights

Critical thoughts pile on top of each other, pulling me down. It takes mental effort to break out of a blue mood, and to pause for a reality check. Are any of these extreme conclusions really true? Hey, I have been down this road before and always come through it okay. It is time to deal with this downward spiral of negativity.

Insight-inspired Actions

I can prepare a list of "transgressors" together with their errors. This is a powerful list, because it provides clues to unmet personal expectations and to options of how to manage them.

As an example, I may return to my journal to record words of forgiveness: Jack, you are doing the best you can and so am I. Jennifer, you are doing the best you can, and so am I.

How This Worked

Withholding judgment opens up new possibilities to build and nurture friendships.

My goal is to achieve a healthy, more peaceful life. Releasing expectations about what "they" should or should not do brings me closer to that goal. When tempted to use judgmental language, I chuckle because I know the opposite response – acceptance – can help make me happy.

Insight Builder

Let's face it: Somebody somewhere is messing up big time and those mistakes can impact you in endless ways: an unresponsive teacher, an insensitive bus driver, a person living down the street with a barking dog, a bumbling clerk at a department store, that gossiping co-worker, a misleading service rep… And those are just shortcomings you may have experienced today.

When you add to the list those who erred last week, or last year, or decades ago… the list of perpetrators can be endless, if we let it grow.

Question

Does memory of another person's transgressions seem to recur when you are feeling a little low? What would be the simplest, least demanding action you could take, in order to release that deadweight from your balloon so that you can soar higher?

———————————

Day~21

What is Your Stress Level?

I sometimes asked students in evening adult education classes to evaluate their current stress levels. Frequently their response was, "It's so - so." Or, "I'm doing okay." I then asked, "Would you be willing to get out of your chair, move to another side of the classroom, wave a magic wand and get beyond "so-so" and just "okay?"

Stress Point

After students had indicated their willingness to change, I asked this: "Suppose you had a way of finding relief from the most frustrating problem you face right now, what might that problem be?" Typical responses suggested they were undergoing heavy duty challenges:

- Commuting an hour and a half is such a waste of time
- I can't seem to lower my credit card debt
- My father is going to need extra care for his memory loss
- My husband is thinking about a divorce

Insights

To bridge the gap between "okay" and real stress relief, let's take a minute to take a stress temperature. Where are you on the spectrum of being totally tense or totally relaxed?

Insight-inspired Actions

Suppose a fist represents tense and anxious - tight as a drum - while an open palm represents complete relaxation – mellow and carefree. Which best describes you at this moment?

To take this idea a bit further, imagine a "Stress Less Scale," with zero indicating completely relaxed and 10 stressed out. Confronted by a stressor, take a minute to approximate your stress temperature. Are you at a low temp? a medium temp? a high temp?

1. Low stress level? At the low end of the scale, you feel a little off balance.

2. At a medium level, you are less tolerant of problems and interruptions.

3. High stress level? You have trouble sleeping due to anxiety, frustration or worry. IBS-like symptoms often flare up, you are consumed by negative thoughts, and you have difficulty finding creative solutions.

Pay close attention to Medium and High Stress levels to discover clues to managing a specific stressor. How do I feel about the situation? What is draining happiness away?

How This Worked

Naming a stressor automatically decreases its power over thoughts and feelings. I no longer walk under a vague dark cloud. Instead, I see stress as a choice point. Do I want to resolve the troublesome issue or not?

If the answer is, Yes! this problem really bothers me, I want to deal with it, there are several options.

I can:

- Change the way I see the problem
- Change the physical circumstances (walk away, close the door)
- Tackle the problem head on, by choosing a direct action, one that will give me peace with the least emotional cost. This can be a phone call, a letter I may not send, or a face-to-face meeting in a neutral setting.

Any of these action steps may change my attitude. And that is actually all that I can control.

Insight Builder

While everyone faces challenges that can trigger a stress response, persistent stress, over months or years, is the most insidious form of stress because the body gradually adapts to imbalance. When students explored their stressors, they were often shocked to discover how extensively stress suppressed their spirits and enjoyment of life. They had adapted to chronic stress unconsciously, and they were relieved to discover they could immediately reverse the process.

Question

Are you willing to assess your stress/unhappiness level before a meal, a meeting with relatives, a doctor's appointment, or a speaking engagement? How can your new awareness to manage stress more effectively help you?

Day~22

Trance Eating?

Have you had one of those "I'm too, too, too!" days? Too tired to think straight, too worried to eat right, too preoccupied with...You name it!

Stress Point

I was at a family gathering which tended to be noisy and frenetic. Perhaps I was 22 at the time. Sitting at the dining table, I happened to glance up at a long mirror above the credenza. I did not recognize the face staring back. Her eyes were vacant, lost in some distant world. Beyond an occasional nod or non-committal "Hmmm," she scarcely participated in the conversation. If she suddenly teleported, would anyone notice?

Insights

I looked down at my empty plate, and was shocked to discover that I could eat without remembering. I had no recollection of eating, beyond a vague aftertaste of lasagna and undoing a notch on the belt of my jeans. Awake? No way. It was more accurate to say my senses were numbed out.

Insight-inspired Actions

Eating while in a self-induced trance was scary. Earth calling Patricia! Anybody home? There has to be a way to stay "awake" at the dinner table. I will rewind the tape and examine it for clues. First clue: Feeling mad, yes, angry. Second clue: Preoccupied with the drama around me. Third clue: A little voice shouting, "Run away," but I can't.

How This Worked

- Anger often follows the stream of negative thoughts I built in my mind. Antidote: How do those negative thoughts help me right now?

- Each person at the dinner table brought his or her own life events, thoughts and feelings. Antidote: I cannot be responsible for others' dramas.

- Detach and disengage from the life around me? Antidote: Consider potential interactions and choose only those that will nurture and fulfill me.

Insight Builder

During those "I'm too exhausted, too angry, too..." moments, we may disengage from life's dramas, and then compensate by overeating and tuning out. In these situations, the wisdom of spiritual masters can be a godsend. They teach that detachment from expectations regarding outcomes differs from hiding or running away from negative thoughts and emotions.

Question

How do you distinguish between detachment from disturbing outcomes and avoiding them? When facing adversity, which technique will you use to remain calm and centered, beyond the siren song of a comfort food?

Day~23

Understanding a "Have to Be On Time" Syndrome

Which is more upsetting: Arriving too early, and sitting around waiting for your opposite number to show up? Or arriving late after an event has started or after someone else has taken your spot? None of the above?

Stress Point

I don't like being late. There, I said it. Whether for a one-on-one meeting, a casual gathering or for a scheduled event, I place a premium on being "on time."

Insights

There are two ways of looking at this. There is rationalizing: tardiness carries a penalty – missed appointments, missed flights-trains-buses, missed exams, missed sales, and so on. And there is illogical thinking: I have to be on time because I'm a bad person if I'm late. There is something else going on. A need to be on time feels as though it is entrenched in my DNA.

Insight-inspired Actions

Improve time management? How much time should I allot for traveling to the dentist via a perennially congested arterial, for the dental hygienist to complete a cleaning, and for the commute back home? I might add a little extra travel time for unexpected delays or inclement weather for a reasonable ETA.

Beyond better time management, being "late" or being "on time" reflects preferences I bring to the table. Punctuality saves me time and energy, reduces stress associated with missing out, and improves interactions with others, all strong pluses. In contrast, being late underscores a lack of commitment to myself, and to others. Conclusion: I'll continue to be on time but without the guilt.

How This Worked

Being "late" and being "on time" carry subjective undertones, don't they? Scheduling is an efficient way to handle personal and business life, bringing order to disorder. Scheduling relies on values and preferences – which tasks are important, and which have the highest priority. Being "late" and being "on time" also reflect personal comfort levels. While a compulsion can drive either behavior, there are no absolute standards of right or wrong.

Insight Builder

Aristotle is quoted as saying, "Man is a rational animal." Perhaps it is more accurate to say that people are rationalizing beings. "There are always two sides to the question" is another old saw. We make choices based on our dynamic world of habits, prejudices, preferences, and "gut feelings," as well as analytical assessments, dispassionately weighing tangible pros and cons.

Being chronically late can lead to consequences beyond missed opportunities. For example, those directly affected by your tardiness may feel resentful, creating a ripple of stress.

Question

Do you have an "on time" or "always a little late" pattern? How does this impact those who have to deal with this pattern?

Day~24

Stress or Burnout? - Why It's Important to Know the Difference

Are stress and burnout the same? Or are they two different consequences of chronic imbalance that can be treated differently?

Stress Point

Scenario 1: Stress symptoms: Tired, feeling blue, frustrated that I cannot quite get free of those persistent, stay awake at night stream of thoughts. However, each day can offer a fresh start.

Scenario 2 follows scenario 1: Stress symptoms: It's one of those, "why bother" days. Whatever I do (or don't do), what difference will it make? Motivated? Are you kidding? I haven't been motivated in a year.

Insights

At first I believed promises that restructuring and reorganization of the company would yield tangible benefits for the corporate family, employees specifically. Then reality set in. The pressure to maintain a quality of excellence was undermined by staff and budget cuts. Who would be laid off next? Physical symptoms – chronic muscle pain and fatigue – increased. Disturbed sleep left me feeling used up. It was getting harder to think about the future.

Insight-inspired Actions

Burnout is a heavy duty problem, requiring a major overhaul to reverse the downward spiral. Number one priority: strengthen my support network of people whom I can rely on, no matter what. Next, refocus on self-care. Burnout weakens my immune system, leaving me vulnerable to infections, chronic disease and premature aging. Third, I need to clarify new work expectations and incentives. And I need adequate resources to meet added responsibilities.

How This Worked

Burnout is stress pushed to the limits. Rather than focusing on successfully completing the task on hand, a sense of failure can be overwhelming. Recognizing burnout and taking corrective steps are critically important to reversing mental and physical exhaustion.

It is time to employ the full spectrum of stress management techniques. Please remember that the most effective overall strategy to relieve stress is holistic: it addresses the physical, mental, spiritual, and emotional aspects of wellness. Facing burnout is an opportune time to re-evaluate your priorities at work and at home for the immediate future and for coming years.

Insight Builder

International surveys have shown that women experiencing job burnout fare worse than their peers financially and health-wise. Burnout is treacherous since women can slowly use up their physical, mental and emotional reserves, without being conscious of it. Burnout is linked to emotional eating, depression, chronic pain, heart disease, high blood pressure, obesity, stroke and substance abuse.

Though traumatic, burnout offers a golden opportunity for a major tune-up. It can be a time to take stock, to revamp diet, exercise and self-care including a comprehensive stress management program. It opens the door to consolidating and refocusing on activities to reach long-term goals.

Question

Viewing burnout as the far end of the stress response spectrum, how close are you to reaching your limits of toleration?

PEACEFUL
MIND

Day~25

Immediate Self-Care? There's an App for That!

Entrepreneurs are capitalizing on the growing popularity of mobile devices such as smart phones, tablets and arm bands to address widespread health concerns. They are designing software to help individuals monitor everything from pulse rate, sleep quality and blood pressure to exposure to UV light from the sun. Will such high tech strategies actually improve self-care?

Stress Point

Does this sound familiar? Like many conscientious people, you do your best to eat right, lose surplus weight that has inexorably crept upward, exercise regularly to reduce stress, stay fit, and get enough sleep. However, your "best" isn't getting you where you want to be, and you feel stuck. You download an app to track your fitness activities. Why stop there? Go ahead and add a sleep tracker, a food checker and a meditation app. Will you use this stuff?

Insights

Anything that can simplify the task of meeting fitness goals is appealing. Theoretically, apps can be inducements to go to the gym more often, to use that piece of exercise equipment purchased months ago, or even to walk more frequently. The common denominator remains the same: devices require the potential user to actually use them. Not just to use them for a day, a week or a month, but to use them regularly as a life-long practice.

Insight-inspired Actions

You can use apps to keep tabs on your workouts, including duration, calories burned, and track running, such as distance traveled, pace and elevation change. You can find popular walking/running paths in your area using the GPS feature of your phone.

A bit overwhelmed, you decide to focus on walking the often recommended 10,000 steps as a fitness goal. You check the device frequently during the day to be sure you are on track for a perfect score. The next day, another perfect score! This is exciting!

How This Worked

After several days, life intrudes. Schedules conflict with regular walking. There are responsibilities at home and at work. Day 4, 5, 8, and 9 go by and you log a thousand steps, not 10,000. Frustration sets in. You resolve to begin tracking again…tomorrow or next week or next month? Is it possible that your app facilitated backsliding?

Insight Builder

Surveys of individuals who have successfully changed health habits, such as sustaining major weight loss for over 5 years, indicate the value of self-monitoring. Logs, journals and a buddy system can help us stay aware of progress and new challenges. But this is only part of the picture.

There are thousands of downloadable software programs that are health-related. Even so, gadgets and apps are not what keep us on track. Alone they are not reliable sources of motivation for permanent lifestyle change. Multiple strategies are needed that encompass not only physical but mental, spiritual and emotional solutions. Social engagement, building a string of successes that enhance self-efficacy and positive reinforcement from a supportive community are also essential.

Question

Do health apps suit your style, or is this trend destined to join last year's treadmill, rowing machine and free weights in an exercise backwater?

Day~26

How to be a Better Problem Solver

Do you believe you are good at dealing with problems, or would you say your problem solving abilities are not so great? In either case, what blocks creative solutions?

Stress Point

Remember the social studies class, when the teacher droned on about the Magna Carta and origins of constitutional democracy? You jotted down 5 pertinent facts, and highlighted textbook facts and figures to be memorized in order to pass the next test. A far cry from creative problem solving!

Insights

Sadly I can count on the fingers of one hand, the number of times I was encouraged in school or college to be more imaginative or creative.

Insight-inspired Actions

How to become a better problem solver?

- Become aware of negative thoughts about limitations: I believe I can accomplish what I set out to do. This is called self-efficacy and it is a potent stress reliever.

- Take more time for self-care: Creativity blooms when I am rested, energized by good nutrition, centered with a spiritual practice, and not held back by thinking "I can't!"

- Build a safe environment to brainstorm your ideas. Nothing stifles imagination faster than ridicule and guilt trips.

- Develop a social support system that recognizes and nurtures all of your talents.

How This Worked

Deciding to unleash imagination/intuition/insight building is an essential step to solving a vast array of problems -- faster and easier. Creative problem solving depends on committing to reclaim the incredible powers we were born with.

Insight Builder

Certainly there are plenty of roadblocks to creative problem solving.

"Only inventors or artists can be creative" - not true! Women and men in professions across the board, have demonstrated the power of insights and novel solutions, whether they are engineers or real estate agents.

"Either you have creativity or you don't" – not true! A vast body of research indicates that insight problem solving can be enhanced, taught, encouraged and used to good effect by children as well as by adults.

"Daydreamers are slackers" - not true! This societal judgment derives from a "work hard" ethic that equates "busy-all-the-time" with maximum productivity and profit. Experience reveals that a simplistic formula does not guarantee life-long success.

Question

Clients often say they don't have enough time to gaze out the window, to daydream, to think about "what ifs." Are you willing to rebalance your schedule in order to create "imagination time?"

———————————

Day~27

The Most Important Fact to Tell Your Doctor?

Doctors and pharmacists are keenly aware of the fact that many patients do not comply with prescribed medications or treatment protocols, regardless of how serious their medical condition. When are patients' attitudes, preferences or emotional state considered?

Stress Point

Scene 1: "You need an MRI scan." I was okay with that, until I saw the narrow opening of the machine she planned to insert me into.

Scene 2: "Your lab results look normal, I recommend you eat more fiber," advised Dr. ABC before abruptly moving on to his next patient.

Scene 3: "What drugs are you currently taking?" and "List any reactions to medications" -- as limited questions on the laborious patient intake form.

Insights

What characterizes the above interactions with medical personnel? None of these people were interested in me! I felt stressed and neglected. Left dangling, fearful of a claustrophobic apparatus. Questioning a vague recommendation about fiber. Doubtful whether the medical staff considered my diet, level of physical activity, use of dietary supplements, or mind/body practices as relevant.

Insight-inspired Actions

At some level there was a violation of trust. I needed to don the shields and powers of a female action heroine, such as Wonder Woman, before a medical appointment.

Steps to be proactive:

- List health concerns that I want addressed.

- Communicate any discomfort or stress associated with the office visit. Repeat as often as needed until staff and physicians acknowledge this.

- Request details to clarify recommended protocols. My agreement depends upon full disclosure of pros and cons, and that I am treated as a full participant in planning a treatment regimen.

How This Worked

Accustomed to a Western medical model, patients generally defer to doctors and other qualified healthcare providers to treat and cure illnesses. This model relies on pharmaceuticals, often invasive procedures and complex diagnostic testing. Efficient clinic operations require streamlined procedures to process patients – a strategy that does not encourage patient interaction.

Furthermore, patients often end up as "a case of atrial fibrillation," "a case of osteoarthritis," or "a case of jaundice," rather than being considered as individuals. By assuming greater responsibility for my own health, I can exert more control of outcomes. As an example, I insist that my stress level and preferences be acknowledged in designing any treatment plan.

Insight Builder

It is astonishing that about 50% of patients throughout the world do not follow their doctor's prescriptions. Although there are multiple reasons for patient non-compliance, patient stress, confusion or distrust play prominent roles.

Patients and concerned individuals motivated to prevent or limit age-related illness often search for answers beyond conventional medical treatment. In body-mind approaches to healing, whether described as integrative medicine or complementary and alternative medicine, stress management is often recognized as an essential ingredient in comprehensive programs for lifestyle change.

Question

Does your primary healthcare provider and her/ his staff treat you as an individual or as an example of an illness/ disease?

PEACEFUL
MIND

Day~28

"My Life is Ruined!"

It is difficult to overemphasize the power of a negative thought. The body reacts to perceptions about stress and "changes" real or not, as if they are actual threats. The consequences on health and well-being can be profound.

Stress Point

1. Carrie must have been all of four years old. Brightly patterned dress, a ribbon in her hair, tiny pearl posts decorated her ears. There she stood with arms folded and scolding Daddy. "I don't like that and I won't do it. My life is ruined!" She stamped her foot and headed for the exit.

2. Rita arrived at my adult education class clearly upset. With all of her 18 year old passion, she exclaimed: "I haven't been able to lose 5 pounds, I won't be able to enter the Daffodil Princess Contest next week. My life is ruined!"

3. Karen looked with dismay at a copy of her reprinted cookbook at the local print shop. Unbelievably, the title page was smeared. The entire order of 1000 copies would have to be reprinted. "I won't be able to fill customer orders. My day is ruined!" She storms out of the receiving area to console herself with comfort food.

Insights

"Disasters" can happen to us at any age. (I am not talking about the life threatening types of disasters so well covered by the media.) Let's consider events that seem to threaten our hopes, dreams, desires and expectations.

Insight-inspired Actions

First question: Are there small and large upsets? My answer is No! They involve the same physiological response. While they may be irrational, upsets are real enough to the body.

Second question: What can I do about extreme negative thoughts, such as a "ruined life?" They squelch creativity and limit productivity. Am I exaggerating, imagining an extreme outcome, or am I refusing to recognize positive counterbalancing factors?

How This Worked

1. As a preschooler, Carrie is too young to understand that her thoughts, words and actions are learned responses, and she lacks the skill set to look objectively at her behavior patterns. However, if Daddy bends down, listens to her upset, and lets her know he understands how she feels about his apparent transgression chances are the storm will quickly pass.

2. If Rita would reconsider her "life is ruined" conclusion, and pay attention to her self-talk, she could challenge this dramatization by recalling how she faced (and survived) similar situations in the past. She might think about how she would support her best friend who wanted to lose weight fast. As a teenager, Rita may have a deeper concern. She may be thinking about her

future beyond a beauty contest. Perhaps she sees a scholarship as a stepping stone for her career.

3. As a business woman and entrepreneur, Karen is well aware of the financial obligations of a successful business. Inevitably there are temporary setbacks. She has kept her company afloat for 3 years. Since most new businesses fold in the first year, she has already beaten the start-up odds. After managing the initial surprise, Karen negotiates a reprint at no cost, and decides to work with another printer with an impeccable track record. She has no need to plunge into old stress responses or resort to comfort food.

Insight Builder

Very often we learned how to respond to unwanted or unpleasant circumstances from childhood role models when we were vulnerable. We were shown, by their words and actions, (such as exclaiming "my life is ruined"), the right way to think. Early indoctrination becomes entrenched and guides behavior as we grow older, whether in personal relationships, home life or work.

Question

Was the most recent challenge you faced a "hassle" or was it a "horror"? What silver lining will change a "my life is ruined" reaction to acceptance and new insights?

PEACEFUL MIND

Day~29

When Friends and Family Become 'Intruders'

Hospitality is often considered a virtue. However, our home has become a very personal space. I have a keen sense of balance between welcoming guests on one hand, and a feeling of being invaded, on the other.

Stress Point

Friends with a large number of children phone to say they will be in the area, and would like to come for a visit. Their call sends me into panic mode. Too many people! The thought of crowding my personal space, including meditation area and home offices, sends me into a downward spiral.

Insights

I enjoy sharing with each child, unique in his way and I miss seeing the children more frequently. Yet boys will be boys, and even indoor soft toys can damage fragile artwork or white leather furniture. Certain areas of our home are very private, indeed they are sanctuaries. The challenge is to protect personal spaces, and at the same time, enjoy the children and offer hospitality.

Insight-inspired Actions

Before the visit, I spread coverlets on leather furniture, hang a "girls only" sign on my bathroom door and relocate several

91

fragile knick-knacks. As the result of relocations over the years, I learned to protect fragile mementoes and heirlooms. We dig up outdoor games and toys, and set up the ping pong table in the backyard. When the boys arrive, I remind them of private areas, and get their buy-in.

How This Worked

In talking with the boys, I express my concerns without blaming anyone. I honor their maturity, and am ready to listen to their feedback. At the same time, we provide plenty of opportunities for the kids to have fun and burn off energy out of doors. We also involve them in meal preparation and in clean up. Assured that personal space will be respected, I relax and completely enjoy these visits.

Insight Builder

As a child I resented relatives who admonished us with commands such as, "Don't touch that! Don't go there! Don't do that." They seemed incapable of understanding that my sister and I were fully able to abide by rules, when we were honored as mature people. We did not require domineering adults to dictate our behavior at any time.

Question

Are there occasions when you feel it is necessary to delineate a personal living space? How does this preference serve you today?

Day~30

An Exercise in Leadership: Setting Up a Support Group

Since ancient times, women have gathered to listen to each other, to speak their truths, and to take action with clear intention. These gatherings provide support for individuals seeking fresh awareness and new insights to help them break free of old, self-limiting patterns.

Stress Point

In my thirties and struggling with negative self-talk, I searched for a support group that would help me improve confidence and self-esteem. I envisioned a loving group of women supporting each other, but none that I joined hit the spot. Moreover, groups I joined – female and mixed groups – created rather than minimized stress. Often one or two people were allowed to dominate, or confidentiality was compromised. Sometimes the group was geared to enabling members, rather than to supporting their growth.

Insights

To remedy various shortcomings, I recommend an Insight Circle based on the premise that no one needs to be changed, that everyone is doing the best she can. Participants do not offer advice or make judgments. There are no rules about lifestyle change -- diets, exercising, or weight management.

There is nothing for participants to push against. Regardless of where a participant is in her process, she never fails.

Insight-inspired Actions

Participants of Insight Circles explore the Stress Less Wellness Blossom to help them break down complex issues into workable chunks, within the four wellness domains – a Healthy Body, a Peaceful Mind, a Vibrant Spirit and Balanced Emotions. They look to the Circle for support in nurturing their unique creativity and new awareness, and in exploring their unique insight solutions.

How This Worked

What features and characteristics distinguish an Insight Circle from other types of support groups?

Group etiquette: Whatever is discussed in the Circle stays there. Participants agree to complete confidentiality in order to ensure mutual trust. Each person is encouraged to speak freely and honestly about issues. No single person dominates the Circle. Circle members share what is true for them. They understand there is no room for criticism within the group. They assume ownership of their thoughts and feelings, without blaming others. They do not offer solutions for other participants: they are aware they do not know what is best for another Circle member.

Insight Builder

Within an Insight Circle, a participant can indicate whether she would like insight-based feedback. As an example: "How do you see yourself differently now?" The Circle thrives with active listening. This involves, looking at the speaker directly, listening with sincere interest to the intent and feelings behind the spoken words. And, being patient and empathic, rather than commiserating! Gripes and complaints have no place here.

Question

How can trusted friends support you unconditionally?

Stop Stress without Overeating
30 Stress Days ~ 30 Insight Solutions

Breaking Free to a HEALTHY BODY

Spark your problem-solving skills to de-stress and get back on track to a Healthy Body. Rediscover how to trust yourself with insight solutions for 30 everyday stressors including:

- Stressed, Sleep-Deprived, or Both?
- Physical Exercise ... Does this mean 'Forever?'
- How to Stop Random Nibbling

Breaking Free to a PEACEFUL MIND

If you have enjoyed this book, please consider leaving a kind review on Amazon to inspire others to Stop Stress without Overeating and Break Free to a Peaceful Mind.

Breaking Free to a VIBRANT SPIRIT

Ready to re-ignite your pilot light to end chronic stress? Discover how to find your own insights to break free to a Vibrant Spirit through self-acceptance, gratefulness, and happiness in thirty chapters such as:

- A 'Tropical Island Paradise' … The Ultimate Stress Solution?
- I'm All Alone – Fact or Fiction?
- How to Turn "Blahs" into 220 Volts

Breaking Free to BALANCED EMOTIONS

If persistent stress leaves you tense, upset and tempted to overeat, Patricia will show you how she used insights to identify feelings, express them in healthy ways and nurture self-care for stress relief that works in thirty chapters such as:

- How to Manage 'Icky' Feelings
- The Gift of Envy
- Is it Okay to Deny Anger?

Patricia A. Ronzio, M.Ed., CHES

Life Coach, Wellness Consultant, Speaker, Author

Helping busy women who are tired of sacrificing their health and happiness to a hectic schedule, Stress Less and Live More!

The founder of New Paradigm Coaching, Patricia has been coaching women for over 15 years. She has an eclectic background that provides a unique breadth to her coaching skills and perspective.

As a participant in the global community, she is sensitive to world cultures and coaches women in many countries. Canadian born and English grown, she realized a childhood dream to become a linguist [French, German and Italian] and traveled extensively throughout Europe.

A former overeater and yoyo dieter, Patricia's life-changing insight that "weight issues" were really "stress issues" was a turning point in her life. Using creative insights for chronic stressors, she eliminated food and weight as roadblocks for

20+ years. Patricia teaches a heart-centered, whole person perspective that combines body, mind, spirit and emotions for life-long wellness.

Patricia has successfully created a deeply nurturing and unconditionally loving relationship with her husband Bob of 24 years. She combines holistic self-care practices to nurture a healthy body, peaceful mind, vibrant spirit, and balanced emotions.

Training and Certifications

M.Ed., Health Education, University Houston
B.A., Antioch University, Seattle
Certified Health Education Specialist [CHES]
Certified Physical Fitness Specialist [CPT]
Holistic Stress Management Instructor [HSMI]
Emotional Freedom Technique Practitioner
Member International Coach Federation
Wellness Councils of America [WELCOA] Faculty
Coach University [Graduate Life Coaching]

Additional Professional Activities:

Wellness Director. For 9 ½ years Patricia directed, designed, implemented and evaluated innovative employee wellness programs for 260 school districts.

Founder, New Paradigm Wellness Consulting. Patricia helps organizations positively impact employee well-being and a culture of health. She employs multilayer skills and corporate experience in program development, education and client service to create long-term solutions.

Co-founder, Insight Learning Institute. With her husband, Robert Ronzio Ph.D., Patricia explores the application of principles of insight learning to promote health, wellness and well-being.

Motivational Speaker. Patricia presents a new model, an insight-based and holistic solution to stress management, and inspires audiences to spark their own creative genius and generate unique and powerful insights to solve difficult, everyday energy drains.

Author. Patricia shares personal insights that arose out of a decades' long struggle with stress and overweight issues in the *Busy Women Stress Less Series™*.

Recent Publication. Insight-motivated Learning: A Model to Improve Stress Management and Adherence in Chronic Health Conditions. *Integrative Medicine: A Clinician's Journal.* April 2012.

Websites:

www.newparadigmcoaching.com

www.insightlearninginstitute.org

www.newparadigmwellnessconsulting.com

Please visit Patricia's website at:

www.newparadigmcoaching.com

Special Relaxation Bonus!

Enjoy an 8 minute audio-v_deo – *Journey into Relaxation* – to calm anxious thoughts and let go of tension.

Frazzled to Free Blog

Sign up for the *Frazzled to Free* blog to receive inspiring articles about stress management, wellness, self-care and weight loss.

Life Coaching

Explore one-on-one coaching by phone or Skype with Patricia in a complimentary 30 minute consultation. Contact her at: coach@newparadigmcoaching.com.